Recov
L o s s

MW00985034

Dale & Juanita Ryan

6 Studies for
Groups or Individuals

With Notes for Leaders

✔ LIFE RECOVERY GUIDES

INTERVARSITY PRESS
DOWNERS GROVE, ILLINOIS 60515

©1990 by Dale and Juanita Ryan

All rights reserved. No part of this book may be reproduced in any form without written permission from InterVarsity Press, P.O. Box 1400, Downers Grove, Illinois 60515.

InterVarsity Press is the book-publishing division of InterVarsity Christian Fellowship, a student movement active on campus at hundreds of universities, colleges and schools of nursing in the United States of America, and a member movement of the International Fellowship of Evangelical Students. For information about local and regional activities, write Public Relations Dept., InterVarsity Christian Fellowship, 6400 Schroeder Rd., P.O. Box 7895, Madison, WI 53707-7895.

All Scripture quotations, unless otherwise indicated, are from the Holy Bible, New International Version. Copyright © 1973, 1978, International Bible Society. Used by permission of Zondervan Bible Publishers.

Cover illustration: Tim Nyberg

ISBN 0-8308-1157-5

Printed in the United States of America

12	11	10	9	8	7	6	5	4
99	98	97	96	95	94	93		

An Invitation to Recovery

Life Recovery Guides are rooted in four basic convictions.

First, we are in need of recovery. The word *recovery* implies that something has gone wrong. Things are not as they should be. We have sinned. We have been sinned against. We are entangled, stuck, bogged down, bound and broken. We need to be healed.

Second, recovery is a commitment to change. Because of this, recovery is a demanding process and often a lengthy one. There are no quick fixes in recovery. It means facing the truth about ourselves, even when that truth is painful. It means giving up our old destructive patterns and learning new life-giving patterns. Recovery means taking responsibility for our lives. It is not easy. It is sometimes painful. And it will take time.

Third, recovery is possible. No matter how hopeless it may seem, no matter how deeply we have been wounded by life or how often we have failed, recovery is possible. Our primary basis for hope in the process of recovery is that God is able to do things which we cannot do ourselves. Recovery is possible because God has committed himself to us.

Finally, these studies are rooted in the conviction that the Bible can be a significant resource for recovery. Many people who have lived through difficult life experiences have had bits of the Bible thrown at their pain as a quick fix or a simplistic solution. As a result, many people expect the Bible to be a barrier to recovery rather than a resource. These studies are based on the belief that the Bible is not a book of quick fixes and simplistic solutions. It is, on the contrary, a practical and helpful resource for recovery.

We were deeply moved personally by these biblical texts as we worked on this series. We are convinced that the God of the Bible can bring serenity to people whose lives have become unmanageable. If you are looking for resources to help you in your recovery, we invite you to study the Bible with an open mind and heart.

Getting the Most from Life Recovery Guides

Life Recovery Guides are designed to assist you to find out for yourself what the Bible has to say about different aspects of recovery. The texts you will study will be thought-provoking, challenging, inspiring and very personal. It will become obvious that these studies are not designed merely to convince you of the truthfulness of some idea. Rather, they are designed to allow biblical truths to renew your heart and mind.

We want to encourage realistic expectations of these discussion guides. First, they are not intended to be everything-the-Bible-says about any subject. They are not intended to be a systematic presentation of biblical theology.

Second, we want to emphasize that these guides are not intended to provide a recovery program or to be a substitute for professional counseling. If you are in a counseling relationship or are involved in a support group, we pray that these studies will enrich that resource. If you are not in a counseling relationship and your recovery involves long-term issues, we encourage you to consider seeking the assistance of a mental health professional.

What these guides are designed to do is to help you study a series of biblical texts which relate to the process of recovery. Our hope is that they will allow you to discover the Good News for people who are struggling to recover.

There are six studies in each Life Recovery Guide. This should provide you with maximum flexibility in how you use these guides. Combining the guides in various ways will allow you to adapt them to your time schedule and to focus on the concerns most important to you or your group.

All of the studies in this series use a workbook format. Space is provided for writing answers to each question. This is ideal for personal study and allows group members to prepare in advance for the discussion. The guides also contain leader's notes with suggestions on how to lead a group discussion. The notes provide additional background information on certain questions, give helpful tips on group dynamics and suggest ways to deal with problems that may arise during the discussion. These features enable someone with little or no experience to lead an effective discussion.

Suggestions for Individual Study

1. As you begin each study, pray that God would bring healing and recovery to you through his Word.

2. After spending time in personal reflection, read and reread the passage to be studied.

3. Write your answers in the spaces provided or in a personal journal. Writing can bring clarity and deeper understanding of yourself and of the Bible. For the same reason, we suggest that you write out your prayers at the end of each study.

4. Use the leader's notes at the back of the guide to gain additional insight and information.

5. Share what you are learning with someone you trust. Recovery is empowered by experiences of community.

Suggestions for Group Study

Even if you have already done these studies individually, we strongly encourage you to find some way to do them with a group of other people as well. Although each person's recovery is different, everyone's recovery is empowered by the mutual support and encouragement that can only be found in a one-on-one or a group setting. Several reminders may be helpful for participants in a group study:

1. Realize that trust grows over time. If opening up in a group setting is risky, realize that you do not have to share more than what feels safe to you. However, taking risks is a necessary part of recovery. So, do participate in the discussion as much as you are able.

2. Be sensitive to the other members of the group. Listen attentively when they talk. You will learn from their insights. If you can, link what you say to the comments of others so the group stays on the topic. Also, be affirming whenever you can. This will encourage some of the more hesitant members of the group to participate.

3. Be careful not to dominate the discussion. We are sometimes so eager to share what we have learned that we do not leave opportunity for others to respond. By all means participate! But allow others to do so as well.

4. Expect God to teach you through the passage being discussed and through the other members of the group. Pray that you will have a profitable time together.

5. We recommend that groups follow a few basic guidelines, and that these guidelines be read at the beginning of each discussion session. The guidelines, which you may wish to adapt to your situation, are:

   a. Anything said in the group is considered confidential and will not be discussed outside the group unless specific permission is given to do so.

   b. We will provide time for each person present to talk if he or she feels comfortable doing so.

   c. We will talk about ourselves and our own situations, avoiding conversation about other people.

   d. We will listen attentively to each other.

   e. We will be very cautious about giving advice.

f. We will pray for each other.

If you are the discussion leader, you will find additional suggestions and helpful ideas for each study in the leader's notes. These are found at the back of the guide.

Recovering from Loss

We have all experienced loss. Each stage of life brings a new set of changes. And each change brings with it unavoidable losses.

We all lose our childhood. We all lose our expectations for parents who are perfect. And, later in life, we lose our hopes that we will be perfect parents ourselves.

Eventually, we find it difficult to avoid a growing consciousness of our limitations. We can't do everything. Every choice we make requires us to turn away from other possibilities. We are limited. And we experience our limitations as a loss.

In a society characterized by both mobility and divorce, most of us have experienced loss of friends or family members. Parents split up. Friends move away.

Death is, of course, the most dramatic loss we anticipate and experience in life. Our parents, our spouse, our children or our friends may die. And we know that we are mortal as well.

The reality of these losses needs to be acknowledged and incorporated into our understanding of ourselves and the world. This is what it means to recover from loss. The process we go through is this particular recovery journey called *grief*.

Grief is not itself something we recover from. It is, rather, a process that helps us to recover from the many losses we experience.

Grief makes it possible for us to face the painful reality of our losses, incorporate those losses into our understanding of life and somehow move on. The purpose of grief is not to help us to forget what we have lost, but to help us grow in understanding, compassion and courage in the midst of our losses.

We all know that grief is emotionally painful work. Grief allows us to heal and to grow, but the cost in emotional energy is often very high. Because of this, we often seek ways to postpone the disciplines of grief. We may tell ourselves: "Look on the bright side." Or, "Keep a smile on your face." But attempts to avoid the emotionally painful process of grief do not lead to growth. In writing about the grief after a death, John Bowlby says:

> For mourning to have a favorable outcome it appears to be necessary for a bereaved person to endure this buffeting of emotion. Only if he can tolerate the pining . . . the seemingly endless examination of how and why the loss occurred, and the anger at anyone who might have been responsible . . . can he come gradually to recognize and accept that the loss is in truth permanent and that his life must be shaped anew.[1]

People who are doing the emotionally painful work of grief need friends who will follow the biblical injunction: "Mourn with those who mourn." And, they need to experience afresh the comforting presence of Jesus who is a "man of sorrows, acquainted with grief."

Our prayer is that in studying these texts you will experience God's comforting presence in your life as he gives you the strength to grieve your losses. "Blessed are those who mourn," Jesus said, "for they will be comforted" (Matthew 5:4).

May your roots sink deeply in the soil of God's love.

Dale and Juanita Ryan

———————

[1]John Bowlby, *Loss* (New York: Basic Books Inc., 1980) p. 93.

1
The God
Who
Grieves

Most of us find it difficult to give ourselves permission to grieve. We are disappointed that it takes us so long to adapt to losses. We are distressed that the emotions involved are so painful. We feel that we should be able to handle it better. We wonder if something is wrong with us.

And we wonder about God. Is God also disappointed by our grief? Does he think we should be over this by now? Will he be distressed that our faith hasn't made us immune to pain? Will he dismiss our pain as faithlessness and say, "Pull yourself together"? Does God understand the process of grief?

It may come as a shock to those of us who have trouble grieving to learn that God grieves. The biblical text for this discussion illustrates that Jesus, who is God with us, wept over the death of his friend and grieved over Jerusalem. The God of the Bible is a God who has himself experienced grief. Out of his personal experience of the pain of grief he is prepared to help us as we grieve.

May focusing on God's grief help you to continue your own process of recovery from loss.

☐ **Personal Reflection** _____

1. What physical responses have you experienced in times of grief?

2. What have your emotional responses been in times of grief?

3. What have your spiritual responses been in times of grief?

☐ **Bible Study**_____

When Jesus saw her weeping, and the Jews who had come along with her also weeping, he was deeply moved in spirit and troubled. "Where have you laid him?" he asked. "Come and see, Lord," they replied. Jesus wept. Then the Jews said, "See how he loved him!" (John 11:33-36)

"O Jerusalem, Jerusalem, you who kill the prophets and stone those sent to you, how often I have longed to gather your children together, as a hen gathers her chicks under her wings, but you were not willing!" (Luke 13:34)

---

1. What insights did you gain during your time of personal reflection?

2. John 11:33-36 describes Jesus' reaction to Mary when she tells him of the death of her brother, and Luke 13:34 describes his sorrow when he is rejected by the people of Jerusalem. How does Jesus' expression of grief in these two stories compare to your own experiences of grief?

3. The focus of Jesus' grief in the passage from John is the death of someone he loved. What, in your experience, is it like to grieve over the loss of someone you love?

4. People interpreted Jesus' weeping as a sign of his love. How do we normally interpret public weeping?

5. Grief is an appropriate response to death. Grief is also an appropriate response to any loss. What is the focus of Jesus' grief in the passage from Luke?

6. In your experience, what is it like to grieve over unfulfilled hopes as Jesus did?

7. What thoughts and feelings do you have as you think about Jesus grieving?

8. How does it help your recovery from loss to know that God grieves?

☐ **Prayer** ————————————————————————

What would you like to say today to the God who has experienced grief?

2
The God
Who Sees
Our Losses

Sometimes our losses go unnoticed. We may minimize the reality of the losses we experience. We may also deny that losses have an emotional impact on us. Or, it may be that we are aware of our loss and the emotional pain that accompanies it, but others do not notice. Other people may downplay the significance of our losses or discount the pain we feel.

For grief to lead to healing and spiritual growth, our losses need to be identified and acknowledged. We need to pay attention to the losses we have experienced. And, we need someone other than ourselves to pay attention as well.

The Bible teaches that God pays attention to our losses. He does not minimize them or deny their reality.

☐ **Personal Reflection** _____

1. Think of a time when you minimized the significance of a loss you experienced. What happened as a result?

2. What experiences have you had of other people minimizing your grief during a time of loss?

How did this effect you?

☐ **Bible Study** ——————————————————————————

When Jesus had again crossed over by boat to the other side of the lake, a large crowd gathered around him while he was by the lake. Then one of the synagogue rulers, named Jairus, came there. Seeing Jesus, he fell at his feet and pleaded earnestly with him, "My little daughter is dying. Please come and put your hands on her so that she will be healed and live." So Jesus went with him.

A large crowd followed and pressed around him. And a woman was there who had been subject to bleeding for twelve years. She had suffered a great deal under the care of many doctors and had spent all she had, yet instead of getting better she grew worse. When she heard about Jesus, she came up behind him in the crowd and touched his cloak, because she thought, "If I just touch his clothes, I will be healed." Immediately her bleeding stopped and she felt in her body that she was freed from her suffering.

At once Jesus realized that power had gone out from him. He turned around in the crowd and asked, "Who touched my clothes?"

"You see the people crowding against you," his disciples answered, "and yet you can ask, 'Who touched me?' "

But Jesus kept looking around to see who had done it. Then the woman, knowing what had happened to her, came and fell at his feet and, trembling with fear, told him the whole truth. He said to her, "Daughter, your faith has healed you. Go in peace and be freed from your suffering." (Mark 5:21-34)

---

1. What insights did you gain during your time of personal reflection?

2. This story shows Jesus' response to two people who had experienced losses. What do we know about the two people and about their losses?

3. What is it about chronic problems or losses like the women in this story experienced that makes them more difficult for us to pay attention to?

4. How does Jesus respond to these people who are in grief?

5. What positive impact do you think Jesus' attention might have had on the woman as she trembled with fear?

6. What thoughts and feelings do you have as you see Jesus' response to these two people who are grieving?

7. Imagine for a moment that you are the woman in this story. Your efforts to get help for your illness have led to more suffering, not less.

You feel lost in the crowd, unworthy of notice. You know that Jesus is on the way to take care of something very important, but you have just enough faith to reach out to touch Jesus as he passes. When you do, you feel yourself being healed. Jesus stops abruptly. He asks the fifty people crowded around him "who touched me?" You sense their confusion. You are afraid. But you tell Jesus what has happened. Listen to what he says: "Your faith has healed you. Go in peace and be freed from your suffering."

What are your thoughts and feelings as you imagine yourself in this story?

8. We often experience God's attentiveness to us through other people who care for us. How has the attentiveness of another person been helpful as you recover from loss?

☐ **Prayer** _____

What loss do you need God to pay attention to?

3
The God Who Hears Us When We Are Depressed

Loss can threaten our identity, our self-esteem and our hope for future happiness. Threats of this kind can result in depression. This may seem obvious, but for most of us it is a difficult reality to accept. It is difficult because depression is uncomfortable for us. It is disruptive to our lives. It is often characterized by crying, disrupted sleep patterns, changes in appetite, social withdrawal, significant spiritual distress and a deep longing for the return of what was lost.

We tend to see depression as a sign either of personal weakness or of spiritual failure. We do not like the way it interferes with our ability to concentrate or to be productive.

How God responds to us when we are depressed is quite important. If he accepts us when we are depressed, then we can cry out to him and expect him to respond. We can tell him about our loss and about our sorrow. If God understands and accepts us when we are depressed, we may be able to find the courage to continue the painful work of grief.

☐ **Personal Reflection** _____

1. What effect does depression have on the way you think and feel about yourself?

2. What has been most helpful to you in times of depression?

☐ **Bible Study** _____

As the deer pants for streams of water,
    so my soul pants for you, O God.
My soul thirsts for God, for the living God.
    When can I go and meet with God?
My tears have been my food day and night,
    while men say to me all day long,
    "Where is your God?"
These things I remember
    as I pour out my soul:
how I used to go with the multitude,
    leading the procession to the house of God,

with shouts of joy and thanksgiving
    among the festive throng.

Deep calls to deep
    in the roar of your waterfalls;
all your waves and breakers
    have swept over me.
By day the LORD directs his love,
    at night his song is with me—
    a prayer to the God of my life.

I say to God my Rock,
    "Why have you forgotten me?
Why must I go about mourning,
    oppressed by the enemy?"
My bones suffer mortal agony
    as my foes taunt me,
saying to me all day long,
    "Where is your God?"

Why are you downcast, O my soul?
    Why so disturbed within me?
Put your hope in God,
    for I will yet praise him,
    my Savior and my God. (Psalm 42:1-4, 7-11)

---

1. What insights did you gain during your time of personal reflection?

2. What signs of depression does the author exhibit?

3. Which of these symptoms are the most difficult for you to accept in yourself?

4. What seems to be the loss that triggered the author's depression?

5. The author seems confused about his relationship with God. What evidence do you see of this confusion?

6. How might depression following a loss lead to this kind of spiritual turmoil?

7. In the midst of his spiritual turmoil, the author is able to talk to God about his feelings of depression. When you are depressed, what is difficult about prayer?

8. How might it be helpful to you to know that God will listen to you and accept you when you are depressed?

9. How can other people be helpful to you when you are depressed and sorrowing over a loss?

☐ **Prayer** _____

What would you like to say to the God who accepts you when you
are depressed?

4
The God
Who Loves
Us When We
Feel Afraid

Fear is one of the most unpleasant emotions that we experience as a part of grief. The experience of loss can create fear in at least two ways. First, an experience of loss creates a sense of immediate danger. We may fear for our well-being or safety. Second, an experience of loss often creates uncertainty about the future. We may fear that other losses will come.

Like depression, fear is seen by many Christians as a kind of spiritual failure. We may hear from others or say to ourselves, "I shouldn't be afraid. I should trust God." Unfortunately, these "shoulds" often create additional fears. We fear that God will reject us because we are afraid. In addition to the initial loss, we must now deal with the complication of perceived losses in our relationship with God.

Fortunately, the Bible is quite straightforward about fear. God knows about our fears. He does not reject us when we are afraid. He is not shocked by our fears. He is not ashamed of us when we are afraid. God still seeks us out, hears our prayers and chooses us to be his people. Even when we are afraid.

☐ Personal Reflection ——————————————————————

1. Think of a loss which you have experienced. What threats of present or future harm did you perceive in this loss?

2. What helped you when you were afraid?

☐ Bible Study——————————————————————————

When the Sabbath was over, Mary Magdalene, Mary the mother of James, and Salome bought spices so that they might go to anoint Jesus' body. Very early on the first day of the week, just after sunrise, they were on their way to the tomb and they asked each other, "Who will roll the stone away from the entrance of the tomb?"

But when they looked up, they saw that the stone, which was very large, had been rolled away. As they entered the tomb, they saw a young man dressed in a white robe sitting on the right side, and they were alarmed.

"Don't be alarmed," he said. "You are looking for Jesus the Nazarene, who was crucified. He has risen! He is not here. See the place where they laid him. But go, tell his disciples and Peter, 'He is going ahead of you into Galilee. There you will see him, just as he told you.'"

Trembling and bewildered, the women went out and fled from the tomb. They said nothing to anyone, because they were afraid. (Mark 16:1-8)

1. What insights did you gain during your time of personal reflection?

2. What losses had these women experienced?

3. What do you imagine they were thinking and feeling on their way to the tomb?

4. In the midst of their grief, they found two unexpected things. First, the stone, which was the focus of their concern, was already rolled away. And, second, a young man commissions them to inform the rest of Jesus' followers of his resurrection. Why do you think

the women responded with fear to these unexpected events?

5. How did the women behave when they were afraid?

6. How does the way the women's fear is described compare with the way you have experienced fear in times of loss?

7. What has been helpful to you when you experience fear in response to loss?

8. Imagine for a moment that God has entrusted you with something which is very important to him. You tremble. You are bewildered. You are afraid. The outcome of your struggle is not at all certain. You prepare yourself to run. You wonder, "Why didn't God entrust this to someone less susceptible to fear?" Reflect for a few moments on the fact that God has a long history of entrusting important tasks to people who struggle with fear.

What thoughts and feelings did you have during this meditation?

☐ **Prayer** ————————————————————————————————

What do you want to say to the God who accepts you when you are afraid?

5
The God
Who Is With Us
When We
Feel Alone

The days immediately after an unexpected loss are often very social times. Friends may reach out to one who has experienced loss for a week or two. The difficult times of loneliness usually come later, when the acute pain of loss is beginning to yield to the longer term pain of the recovery process.

Loneliness can be a very significant struggle during this time. People don't know what to say. They may say foolish things, or inappropriately cheerful things. Friends may try to find meaning in our loss long before we are prepared to entertain such thoughts. Or they may ignore us all together. C. S. Lewis experienced this isolation after the death of his wife. He wrote:

> An odd by-product of my loss is that I'm aware of being an embarrassment to everyone I meet. At work, at the club, in the street, I see people, as they approach me, trying to make up their minds whether they'll "say something about it" or not. . . . Perhaps the bereaved ought to be isolated in special settlements like lepers.[1]

Although grief can leave us feeling very alone, it is the consistent testimony of the Bible that God reaches out to us in times when we are alone. He does not abandon people who struggle with loneliness as part of their recovery from loss.

☐ **Personal Reflection** ————————————————

1. What have other people done or said in response to your grief that has left you feeling alone?

2. What have people done or said in response to your grief that has left you feeling comforted?

☐ **Bible Study**————————————————

I cry aloud to the LORD:
    I lift up my voice to the LORD for mercy.
I pour out my complaint before him;
    before him I tell my trouble.

When my spirit grows faint within me,
    it is you who know my way.
In the path where I walk
    men have hidden a snare for me.
Look to my right and see;
    no one is concerned for me.
I have no refuge;
    no one cares for my life.

I cry to you, O LORD;
    I say, "You are my refuge,
    my portion in the land of the living."
Listen to my cry,
    for I am in desperate need;
rescue me from those who pursue me,
    for they are too strong for me.
Set me free from my prison,
    that I may praise your name.
Then the righteous will gather about me
    because of your goodness to me. (Psalm 142)

---

1. What insights did you gain during your time of personal reflection?

2. The author says, "No one is concerned for me. . . . No one cares for my life." What experiences have you had with feeling alone with your grief?

3. The author says his need is "desperate." What is it like to feel alone with a desperate need?

4. The author asks of God: "Set me free from my prison." In what way can loneliness after a loss be like a prison?

5. In spite of experiencing loneliness, desperation and hopelessness, the author says he has experienced God's presence. He says of God "it is you who know my way," and "you are my refuge." How do your experiences compare with those of the author?

6. The author pours out his complaint and tells his troubles to God. How can prayer be helpful in times of isolation?

7. The author ends by expressing the desire that he be set free from his prison to experience again the joys of a supportive, loving community ("the righteous will gather about me"). Why is it so important for us to eventually break out of our isolation?

What practical steps could we take to move out of our isolation?

8. —I will not leave you as orphans; I will come to you. (John 14:18)
—My presence will go with you and I will give you rest. (Exodus 33:14)
—Surely I am with you always, to the very end of the age. (Matthew 28:20)
One of the central themes of the Bible is "God with Us." Pick one of the above texts which emphasize God's presence with us, meditate on the text in the context of your present circumstances and write

a short prayer asking God to be with you in your recovery.

☐ **Prayer** ─────────────────────────────────────

What would you like to say to God who is with you when you feel alone?

─────────────

[1]C. S. Lewis, *A Grief Observed* (London: Faber and Faber, 1961), pp. 12-13.

6
The God
Who Offers
Healing

Grief is not an ending or a walking away from what we have lost.
Forgetting the person or the dream that died is not the same as
recovery from loss. Recovery from loss allows us to reshape our
relationship with the person or the dream we have lost and to find
ways to grow in our new circumstances.

One of the most demanding challenges of grief involves reinvest-
ing in life. New relationships, new dreams are offered to us. New joy
is possible. That which is new, however, may feel very uncomfortable. We may feel it is somehow wrong to experience the joys of life
again. We will be acutely aware that any time we open ourselves to
new love or to new hope that we also open ourselves to the possibility
of new loss.

The writer of this text experienced God to be very helpful in
learning to experience joy again. He says God has "clothed me with
joy." The same God who understands and accepts our fear, depression and loneliness invites us to reinvest in life.

☐ **Personal Reflection** ——————————————

1. What might make it difficult for you to reinvest in life after a significant loss?

2. What might help you to reinvest in life?

☐ **Bible Study**———————————————————

I will exalt you, O LORD,
> for you lifted me out of the depths
> and did not let my enemies gloat over me.
O LORD my God, I called to you for help
> and you healed me.
O LORD, you brought me up from the grave;
> you spared me from going down into the pit.
Sing to the LORD, you saints of his;
> praise his holy name.
For his anger lasts only a moment,
> but his favor lasts a lifetime;
weeping may remain for a night,
> but rejoicing comes in the morning.

When I felt secure, I said,
    "I will never be shaken."
O LORD, when you favored me,
    you made my mountain stand firm;
but when you hid your face,
    I was dismayed.

To you, O LORD, I called;
    to the Lord I cried for mercy:
"What gain is there in my destruction,
    in my going down into the pit?
Will the dust praise you?
    Will it proclaim your faithfulness?
Hear, O LORD, and be merciful to me;
    O LORD, be my help."

You turned my wailing into dancing;
    you removed my sackcloth and
        clothed me with joy,
that my heart may sing to you and not be silent.
    O LORD my God, I will give you thanks forever.
    (Psalm 30)

---

1. What insights did you gain during your time of personal reflection?

2. The author recalls a time when his grief was so intense that he thought he was going to die. What is it about grief that can make a person feel this way?

3. The text refers to a time when the author believed God hid his face. He also describes this time as a time when his heart was silent—unable to sing to God. During your recovery from loss, what experiences have you had of feeling at a distance from God or of feeling unable to sing to God?

4. In reflecting on his grief, the author also remembers a time when God favored him. During your recovery from loss, what experiences have you had of God's special attention?

5. The author says that "weeping may remain for a night, but rejoicing comes in the morning." How can it be helpful in recovery from loss to know that weeping will not last forever?

6. The author uses a series of metaphors to describe what God had done for him. He says to God: "You lifted me. You brought me up. You healed me. You spared me from going into the pit." Which of these metaphors best describes what you want most from God at this point in recovery?

7. What healing and growth have you experienced as a result of your recovery from loss?

8. The author pictures God as one who can turn "wailing into dancing" and who can replace the clothes of mourning with clothes of joy. Imagine for a moment that you are completely aware of your loss and all that it means. Imagine that you are dressed in black and have been weeping for a long time. Finally, your tears stop. You are able to see God standing in front of you. He offers you new clothes to put on. He invites you to dance.

What response did you have to this image?

☐ **Prayer** _____

What "clothes of mourning" would you like God to turn into "clothes of joy"?

Leader's Notes

You may be experiencing a variety of feelings as you anticipate leading a group using a Life Recovery Guide. You may feel inadequate and afraid of what will happen. If this is the case, know you are in good company. Many of the kings, prophets and apostles in the Bible felt inadequate and afraid. Many other small group leaders share the experience of fear as well.

Your willingness to lead, however, is a gift to the other group members. It might help if you tell them about your feelings and ask them to pray for you. Keep in mind that the other group members share the responsibility for the group. And realize that it is God's work to bring insight, comfort, healing and recovery to group members. Your role is simply to provide guidance for the discussion. The suggestions listed below will help you to provide that guidance.

Using the Life Recovery Guide Series

This Life Recovery Guide is one in a series of eight guides. The series was designed to be a flexible tool that can be used in various combinations by individuals and groups—such as support groups, Bible studies and Sunday-school classes. Each guide contains six studies. If all eight guides are used, they can provide a year-long curriculum series. Or if the guides are used in pairs, they can provide studies for a quarter (twelve weeks).

We want to emphasize that all of the guides in this series are designed to be useful to anyone. Each guide has a specific focus, but all are written with a general audience in mind. Additionally, the workbook format allows for personal interaction with biblical truths, making the guides adaptable to each individual's unique journey in recovery.

The four guides which all individuals and groups should find they can most easily relate to are *Recovery from Distorted Images of God, Recovery from Loss, Recovery from Bitterness* and *Recovery from Shame.* All of us need to replace our distorted images of God with biblically accurate images. All of us experience losses, disappointments and disillusionment in life, as well as loss through death or illness. We all have life experiences and relationships which lead to bitterness and which make forgiveness difficult. And we all experience shame and its debilitating consequences.

The four other guides are *Recovery from Codependency, Recovery from Family Dysfunctions, Recovery from Abuse* and *Recovery from Addictions.* Although these guides have a more specific focus, they address issues of very general concern both within the Christian community and in our culture as a whole. The biblical resources will be helpful to your recovery even if you do not share the specific concerns which these guides address.

Individuals who are working on a specific life issue and groups with a shared focus may want to begin with the guide which relates most directly to their concerns. Survivors of abuse, for example, may want to work through *Recovery from Abuse* and follow it with *Recovery from Shame.* Adult children from dysfunctional families may want to begin with *Recovery from Family Dysfunctions* and then use *Recovery from Distorted Images of God.* And those who struggle with addictive patterns may want to begin with *Recovery from Addictions* and then use *Recovery from Codependency.*

There are many other possibilities for study combinations. The short descriptions of each guide on the last page, as well as the information on the back of each guide will help you to further decide which guides will be most helpful to your recovery.

Preparing to Lead

1. Develop realistic expectations of yourself as a small group leader. Do not feel that you have to "have it all together." Rather, commit yourself to an ongoing discipline of honesty about your own needs. As you grow in honesty about your own needs, you will grow as well in your capacity for compassion, gentleness and patience with yourself and with others. As a leader, you can encourage an atmosphere of honesty by being honest about yourself.

2. Pray. Pray for yourself and your own recovery. Pray for the group members. Invite the Holy Spirit to be present as you prepare and as you meet.

3. Read the study several times.

4. Take your time to thoughtfully work through each question, writing out your answers.

5. After completing your personal study, read through the leader's notes for the study you are leading. These notes are designed to help you in several ways. First, they tell you the purpose the authors had in mind while writing the study. Take time to think through how the questions work together to accomplish that purpose. Second, the notes provide you with additional background information or comments on some of the questions. This information can be useful if people have difficulty understanding or answering a question. Third, the leader's notes can alert you to potential problems you may encounter during the study.

6. If you wish to remind yourself during the group discussion of anything mentioned in the leader's notes, make a note to yourself below that question in your study guide.

Leading the Study

1. Begin on time. You may want to open in prayer, or have a group member do so.

2. Be sure everyone has a study guide. Decide as a group if you want people to do the study on their own ahead of time. If your time together is limited, it will be helpful for people to prepare in advance.

3. At the beginning of your first time together, explain that these studies are meant to be discussions, not lectures. Encourage the members of the group to participate. However, do not put pressure on those who may be hesitant to speak during the first few sessions. Clearly state that people do not need to share anything they do not feel safe sharing. Remind people that it will take time to trust each other.

4. Read aloud the group guidelines listed in the front of the guide. These commitments are important in creating a safe place for people to talk and trust and feel.

5. The covers of the Life Recovery Guides are designed to incorporate both symbols of the past and hope for the future. During your first meeting, allow the group to describe what they see in the cover and respond to it.

6. Read aloud the introductory paragraphs at the beginning of the discussion for the day. This will orient the group to the passage being studied.

7. The personal reflection questions are designed to help group members focus on some aspect of their experience. Hopefully, they will help group members to be more aware of the frame of reference and life experience which they bring to the study. The personal reflection section can be done prior to the group meeting or as the first part of the meeting. If the group does not prepare in advance, approximately ten minutes will be needed for individuals to consider these questions.

The personal reflection questions are not designed to be used directly for group discussion. Rather, the first question in the Bible study section is intended to give group members an opportunity to reveal what they feel safe sharing from their time of personal reflection.

8. Read the passage aloud. You may choose to do this yourself, or prior to the study you might ask someone else to read.

9. As you begin to ask the questions in the guide, keep several things in mind. First, the questions are designed to be used just as they are written. If you wish, you may simply read them aloud to the group. Or you may prefer to express them in your own words. However, unnecessary rewording of the questions is not recommended.

Second, the questions are intended to guide the group toward understanding and applying the main idea of the study. You will find the purpose of each study described in the leader's notes. You should try to understand how the study questions and the biblical text work together to lead the group in that direction.

There may be times when it is appropriate to deviate from the study guide. For example, a question may have already been answered. If so, move on to the next question. Or someone may raise an important question not covered in the guide. Take time to discuss it! The important thing is to use discretion. There may be many routes you can travel to reach the goal of the study. But the easiest route is usually the one we have suggested.

10. Don't be afraid of silence. People need time to think about the question before formulating their answers.

11. Draw out a variety of responses from the group. Ask, "Who else has some thoughts about this?" or "How did some of the rest of your respond?" until several people have given answers to the question.

12. Acknowledge all contributions. Try to be affirming whenever possible. Never reject an answer. If it seems clearly wrong to you, ask, "Which part of the text led you to that conclusion?" or "What do the rest of you think?"

13. Realize that not every answer will be addressed to you, even though this will probably happen at first. As group members become more at ease, they will begin to interact more effectively with each other. This is a sign of a healthy discussion.

14. Don't be afraid of controversy. It can be very stimulating. Differences can enrich our lives. If you don't resolve an issue completely, don't be frustrated. Move on and keep it in mind for later. A subsequent study may resolve the problem. Or, the issue may not be resolved—not all questions have answers!

15. Stick to the passage under consideration. It should be the source for answering the questions. Discourage the group from unnecessary cross-referencing. Likewise, stick to the subject and avoid going off on tangents.

16. Periodically summarize what the group has said about the topic. This helps to draw together the various ideas mentioned and gives continuity to the study. But be careful not to use summary statements as an opportunity to give a sermon!

17. During the discussion, feel free to share your own responses. Your honesty about your own recovery can set a tone for the group to feel safe in sharing. Be careful not to dominate the time, but do allow time for your own needs as a group member.

18. Each study ends with a time for prayer. There are several ways to handle this time in a group. The person who leads each study could lead the group in a prayer or you could allow time for group participation. Remember that some members of your group may feel uncomfortable about participating in public prayer. It might be helpful to discuss this with the group during your first meeting and to reach some agreement about how to proceed.

19. Realize that trust in a group grows over time. During the first couple meetings, people will be assessing how safe they will feel in the group. Do not be discouraged if people share only superficially at first. The level of trust will grow slowly but steadily.

Listening to Emotional Pain

Life Recovery Guides are designed to take seriously the pain and struggle that is part of life. People will experience a variety of emotions during these studies. Your role as group leader is not to act as a professional counselor. Instead it is to be a friend who listens to emotional pain. Listening is a gift you can give to hurting people. For many, it is not an easy gift to give. The following suggestions can help you listen more effectively to people in emotional pain.

1. Remember that you are not responsible to take the pain away. People in helping relationships often feel that they are being asked to make the other person feel better. This is usually related to the helper's own patterns of not being comfortable with painful feelings.

2. Not only are you not responsible to take the pain away, one of the things people need most is an opportunity to face and to experience the pain in their lives. They have usually spent years denying their pain and running from it. Healing can come when we are able to face our pain in the presence of someone who cares about us. Rather than trying to take the pain away, commit yourself to listening attentively as it is expressed.

3. Realize that some group members may not feel comfortable with expressions of sadness or anger. You may want to acknowledge that such emotions are uncomfortable, but remind the group that part of recovery is to learn to feel and to allow others to feel.

4. Be very cautious about giving answers and advice. Advice and answers may make you feel better or feel competent, but they may also minimize peoples' problems and their painful feelings. Simple solutions rarely work, and they can easily communicate "You should be better now" or "You shouldn't really be talking about this."

5. Be sure to communicate direct affirmation any time people talk about their painful emotions. It takes courage to talk about our pain because it creates anxiety for us. It is a great gift to be trusted by those who are struggling.

The following notes refer to the questions in the Bible study portion of each study:

Study 1. The God Who Grieves. John 11:33-36; Luke 13:34.
Purpose: To understand that God also has experienced grief.
Question 2. Jesus wept publicly at a friend's funeral. He also expressed a deep grief-like longing over the rejection he had experienced. We are less likely to express our grief openly.

Question 3. Grief is a time of deep, intense emotions. The passage says that Jesus was "deeply moved and troubled in spirit." Give the group an opportunity to share what their own experiences have been with major losses of people close to them through death, divorce or other circumstances.

Question 4. Weeping in public is interpreted by many people as a sign of weakness. It seems overly-emotional to us. We value the ability to be strong in times of grief and the ability to be self-controlled.

Some people may also think of public weeping as being manipulative, like a fundraising technique used by TV evangelists. As a culture, we do not value or give permission for or trust the open expression of genuine grief.

Question 5. Jesus' grief here is a response to rejection; he is grieving the loss of a potential relationship.

Question 6. Losses of this kind are not usually as tangible as the losses experienced after the death of someone you love. The emotional substance may be just as intense, but we may feel less permission to feel these emotions. There is usually less social support for the grief process, and we may be confused that we are experiencing these emotions at all.

A primary emotional response to unfulfilled expectations is the experience of a deep longing. Notice as well the evidence of anger and sadness in this text. This anger is difficult because it is anger at someone you love, someone with whom you long to have a relationship. The sadness is also difficult because you can't make it better no matter how hard you try. Encourage group members to talk about their experiences with unfulfilled expectations in relationships (for example, with parents, siblings, friends).

Study 2. The God Who Sees Our Losses. Mark 5:21-34.
Purpose: To understand that God is attentive to our losses.
Question 2. Two people in this story are grieving. Jairus, a religious

leader, is experiencing anticipatory loss because his daughter is dying. The woman's losses are related to a chronic illness and the ineffective medical care which had left her in poverty. Part of the dramatic intensity of this story is the assumed uncertainty about whether Jesus can be attentive to both the needs of a wealthy leader of the religious community in acute grief and the needs of a chronically ill and impoverished woman.

Question 3. We all understand acute losses. We understand emergencies. They come with an adrenalin rush that helps us to get ready to respond. Our response to chronic problems, however, is not adrenalin-assisted. We get tired of hearing about it and wonder why the person isn't better yet. We may even find ourselves blaming persons who seem to be chronically needy for their problems. Paying attention to our own problems or to other people's problems is demanding. As a consequence, we may simply choose not to pay attention at all.

Question 4. Jesus listens to Jairus and he responds. He goes with him. The dramatic center of this story is when Jesus pays attention to the impoverished woman even in a crowd of people, even on the way to care for what we might think are the important or acute needs. He pays attention to what has happened. He seeks out the woman to give her individual attention, acknowledgment and blessing.

Question 5. Jesus' attention allowed her to experience his love and interest in her. It took her beyond a physical healing to an emotional/spiritual healing.

Study 3. The God Who Hears Us When We Are Depressed. Psalm 42:1-4, 7-11.
Purpose: To realize that God accepts us when we experience depression in response to loss.

Question 2. He is crying, unable to sleep and unable to eat. He is thinking about his loss and has physical pains ("my bones suffer").

He is also trying to talk himself out of his depression. These are all common symptoms of depression.

Question 4. The author remembers a time when he was a leader of worship. Apparently he is now unable to even go to the temple. Instead of being the leader of "shouts of joy and thanksgiving" he must listen to the voices of his enemies saying, "Where is your God?"

Question 5. The author talks about his longing for God and his sense of separation from God. Yet he affirms God's constant love and presence with him. In one sentence he can say, "God is my Rock," and then ask of God "Why have you forgotten me?"

This kind of spiritual struggle is common in the depression that accompanies grief. During depression, God may feel distant at some times and very close at others. The author's confusion is not merely an intellectual uncertainty but a struggle to make sense out of his faith in light of his loss. The heart of the matter is not a philosophical question about God but rather a question about his personal relationship with God.

Question 6. Part of depression is the realization that God did not protect you from the loss. It may make you wonder who God is. You might ask, "Does God care about me?" Depression can also make you wonder if there is something wrong with you. You might ask, "Was my faith inadequate?" Christians often see depression as a sign of spiritual weakness or failure. They feel that they should be full of hope and joy, ready to accept everything including losses as God's will. Like the author, we may think, "God is not pleased with my sadness. I need to get over these feelings or he will not be pleased with me."

Question 7. It is difficult because we are unsure of God. We worry that he might reject us. Depression makes us withdraw. We may not want to talk to anybody—including God.

Be sensitive to the fact that people in your group may feel guilty about their inability to pray when depressed. Rather than reinforcing this guilt, recognize that seasons of prayerlessness may be unavoidable. Alternatives at such times include asking others to pray for you, waiting in silence before God and allowing biblical passages, such as this psalm, to give voice to your longing for God.

Study 4. The God Who Loves Us When We Feel Afraid. Mark 16:1-8.

Purpose: To realize that God loves us when we experience fear in response to loss.

Question 2. Jesus had died. They had lost a personal friend, the one in whom they had placed all their trust. Any hope that Jesus would be the one to establish God's kingdom had been destroyed.

Question 3. The immediate experience after a great loss is numbness. As a result, the women were probably focused on the very concrete tasks of caring for Jesus' body. Just beneath the surface of this emotional-Novocain effect, however, lay all the emotions of grief.

They must certainly have been confused. They may have been afraid for their personal safety. The male disciples had already fled, and there was good reason for them to think that they themselves might be at risk. They no doubt felt disoriented spiritually and overcome by sadness. It must have seemed that evil would get the last word.

Question 4. Some people may think that fear is a paradoxical response to the resurrection. Shouldn't rejoicing have been the immediate response? Jesus was alive. His kingdom was not defunct! For people in grief, however, good news takes time to settle in. Even people who are followers of Jesus, like the women in this story, may be so disoriented by grief that they are unable to fully appreciate God's power.

Fear can result either from a present threat of harm or a future possibility of harm. The women may have perceived a present threat because they didn't know who the "young man" speaking to them was. They may also have perceived a possibility of harm in the future because they did not understand the implications of this event.

Question 5. Fear often keeps us from doing the things we really want to do. The women fled and were silent. Our best manuscripts of the book of Mark show the book ending here. What high drama! The good news of God's kingdom is entrusted to those who tremble, are bewildered and are afraid. What a risky venture!

The point is not that we should say, "Shame on these weak women who should have rejoiced and acted courageously." Instead, we are to rejoice because God really does entrust his kingdom to us, even though we are afraid. God can apparently tolerate the suspense. He has a long history of entrusting his concerns to people who experience fear. We know from other texts that the women eventually find the courage to speak. We would not know about these events if they kept silence for ever!

Study 5. The God Who Is With Us When We Feel Alone. Psalm 142.

Purpose: To realize that God is with us when we feel alone with our grief.

Question 3. Loneliness can increase the fear that comes with loss. When we are alone with loss, we may feel cut off from the resources and support that we need. Not infrequently, people report concerns that they feel like they are going crazy because they do not get the kind of feedback from others that would help them to evaluate their experiences. Panic is also a common response to being alone with a desperate need.

Question 4. In addition to making us feel more desperate and afraid, isolation can contribute to a sense of hopelessness. We may feel trapped—unable to make any progress on our own. It may feel like there is no way to recover from this painful loss.

Question 5. It is important to acknowledge that some people may not be aware of experiencing God's presence in any meaningful way at this point in their recovery. Other people may have specific examples of how God has been with them during their grief.

The author is experiencing the contrast between social isolation and the comforting presence of God. Notice that experiencing God's presence does not take all the pain away. The author goes back and forth between saying, "I have no refuge," and "You are my refuge." This is an expression of the paradox or the emotional rollercoaster of grief.

Question 6. When no one can or will listen, God listens. When we can't speak, God will listen even more carefully. His Spirit will hear the deep groanings of our hearts, and he will know how we feel.

Prayer is part of the recovery process. Forced or ritualized prayers are not helpful in recovery, but prayers that give voice to real experience are healing. Your prayers will be heard by God, no matter how inarticulate, muddled or confusing they seem as you pray.

It is very painful to be socially isolated. But it is even more painful to be fundamentally alone in life. Christians are deeply committed to the notion that we are not alone. Prayer is testimony to, and an acting out of, this reality.

Question 7. We need other people to help us in our recovery from loss. The author knew this. God knows this. The goal of recovery is not merely to become a stronger individual but to become a person made stronger by the love and support of other people who also struggle towards recovery.

Question 8. Practical steps to move out of the isolation of grief might include (a) finding a grief recovery support group, (b) getting help from a counselor or pastor and (c) reaching out to friends and asking for their support.

Study 6. The God Who Offers Healing. Psalm 30.

Purpose: To understand that God offers healing which makes it possible for us to reinvest in life.

Question 2. It is not uncommon during grief to feel like we want to die because life is not worth living. All hope may seem to be gone. The loss may so deplete our resources for daily living that even the smallest of chores seems impossible. Physically, emotionally and spiritually, grief can be a very debilitating experience.

Question 3. The author is not concerned with theological abstractions. He is accurately remembering the alienation that comes with grief. It may not be easy to listen to his account of experiencing God's absence, but it is often part of grief and little progress will be made in recovery if it is ignored.

Emphasize to the group that, like any healthy relationship, our relationship with God is rooted in covenants more fundamental than "how we are feeling right now about the relationship." God is always with us, no matter how we feel. Therefore, experiences of God's absence do not necessarily indicate spiritual failure or unfaithfulness in our relationship with God. They are a normal part of grief.

Question 4. Many people find that there are times during the process of grief when they experience God's presence in unexpected ways. Sometimes intense and painful experiences of God's absence alternate with remarkable experiences of God's presence. Many people find this kind of spiritual rollercoaster to be very confusing. It is, however, probably an unavoidable counterpart to the emotional rollercoaster which accompanies grief. God's commitments to us are foundational to life. God is not involved just for the short term. He is a relentless, tenacious, persistent lover. His commitments will not change with the emotional or spiritual ups and downs of our lives. He is committed to us for the long haul.

Question 5. There is hope. Grief has a natural course. It does not go on indefinitely. And, because of God's active involvement in our lives, it is even possible to grow when in grief. Hope, however, is easily trivialized.

The author is not minimizing the trauma by saying, "It's not so bad," or "You'll get over it." He is not distracting attention from the trauma by saying "look on the bright side." He is not attempting to truncate the emotional pain by saying "thank God for the loss." He is, however, testifying from his own experience that God is helpful to people who experience losses. When we allow ourselves to feel the depth of our pain and sorrow, we will also be able to feel the full extent of joy that comes with recovery.

For more information about Christian resources for people in recovery and subscription information for STEPS, *the newsletter of the National Association for Christian Recovery, we invite you to write to:*

The National Association for Christian Recovery
P.O. Box 11095
Whittier, California 90603

LIFE RECOVERY GUIDES FROM INTER-VARSITY PRESS
By Dale and Juanita Ryan

Recovery from Abuse. Does the nightmare of abuse ever end? After emotional, verbal and/ or physical abuse how can you develop secure relationships? Recovery is difficult but possible. This guide will help you turn to God as you put the broken pieces of your life back together again. Six studies, 64 pages, 1158-3.

Recovery from Addictions. Addictions have always been part of the human predicament. Chemicals, food, people, sex, work, spending, gambling, religious practices and more can enslave us. This guide will help you find the wholeness and restoration that God offers to those who are struggling with addictions. Six studies, 64 pages, 1155-9.

Recovery from Bitterness. Sometimes forgiveness gets blocked, stuck, restrained and entangled. We find our hearts turning toward bitterness and revenge. Our inability to forgive can make us feel like spiritual failures. This guide will help us find the strength to change bitterness into forgiveness. Six studies, 64 pages, 1154-0.

Recovery from Codependency. The fear, anger and helplessness people feel when someone they love is addicted can lead to desperate attempts to take care of, or control, the loved one. Both the addicted person's behavior and the frenzied codependent behavior progress in a destructive downward spiral of denial and blame. This guide will help you to let go of over-responsibility and entrust the people you love to God. Six studies, 64 pages, 1156-7.

Recovery from Distorted Images of God. In a world of sin and hate it is difficult for us to understand who the God of love is. These distortions interfere with our ability to express our feelings to God and to trust him. This guide helps us to identify the distortions we have and to come to a new understanding of who God is. Six studies, 64 pages, 1152-4.

Recovery from Family Dysfunctions. Dysfunctional patterns of relating learned early in life affect all of our relationships. We trust God and others less than we wish. This guide offers healing from the pain of the past and acceptance into God's family. Six studies, 64 pages, 1151-6.

Recovery from Loss. Disappointment, unmet expectations, physical or emotional illness and death are all examples of losses that occur in our lives. Working through grief does not help us to forget what we have lost, but it does help us grow in understanding, compassion and courage in the midst of loss. This guide will show you how to receive the comfort God offers. Six studies, 64 pages, 1157-5.

Recovery from Shame. Shame is a social experience. Whatever its source, shame causes people to see themselves as unloveable, unworthy and irrreparable. This guide will help you to reform your self-understanding in the light of God's unconditional acceptance. Six studies, 64 pages, 1153-2.